COUNTRY INSIGHTS
DENMARK

Ole Steen Hansen

KT-421-248

LANARK LIBRARY
DISCARDED

WAYLAND

COUNTRY INSIGHTS

BRAZIL • CHINA • CUBA • CZECH REPUBLIC • DENMARK • FRANCE INDIA • JAMAICA • JAPAN • KENYA • MEXICO • PAKISTAN

GUIDE TO THIS BOOK

As well as telling you about the whole of Denmark, this book looks closely at the city of Århus and the village of Hyllested.

This city symbol will appear at the top of the page and information boxes each time the book looks at Århus.

This rural symbol will appear each time the book looks at Hyllested.

C40265700-

SOUTH LANARKSHIRE LIBRARIES

Cover: Almost every Danish child owns a bicycle. Bicycles are more a type of transport than a piece of sports equipment in Denmark.

Title Page: Girls rowing a boat on a lake in one of Denmark's popular leisure parks, on Bornholm Island.

Contents page: Playing ice hockey on a frozen lake in Grenå. The ice should be at least 13 cm thick before anyone attempts to have fun on it.

Series and book editor: Polly Goodman
Designer: Tim Mayer
Consultant: Anne Marley, Principal Librarian, Children & Schools Library Service, Hampshire.

First published in 1997 by
Wayland Publishers Ltd
61 Western Road, Hove
East Sussex, BN3 1JD, England

© Copyright 1997 Wayland Publishers Ltd

Find Wayland on the Internet at http://wayland.co.uk

British Library Cataloguing in Publication Data
Hansen, Ole Steen
  Denmark.– (Country Insights)
  1. Denmark – Juvenile literature
  I. Title
  948.9'059

ISBN 0 7502 2113 5

Typeset by Tim Mayer.
Printed and bound in Italy by LEGO S.p.A., Vicenza.

Contents

Introducing Denmark

Denmark is the smallest and most southerly of the countries of Scandinavia, which lie in northern Europe. It is probably best known for the fairy tales of Hans Christian Andersen, and for being home to the powerful Viking raiders, 1,000 years ago. Denmark is a small country, with limited natural resources. Nevertheless, it has become one of the five richest countries in the world.

A thousand years ago, Danish Vikings conquered and controlled large areas of northern Europe. But since then, Denmark has lost many wars and has been occupied by other nations several times. Today, it is one of the smallest countries in Europe, with a population smaller than London's. Its capital city is Copenhagen.

Denmark has its own distinctive traditions and a tongue-twisting language, which includes several different dialects. Although Denmark is a member of the European Union (EU), recently it has been reluctant to work more closely with the EU and give up some of its independence.

The city of Copenhagen, the capital of Denmark. Copenhagen has few very high buildings.

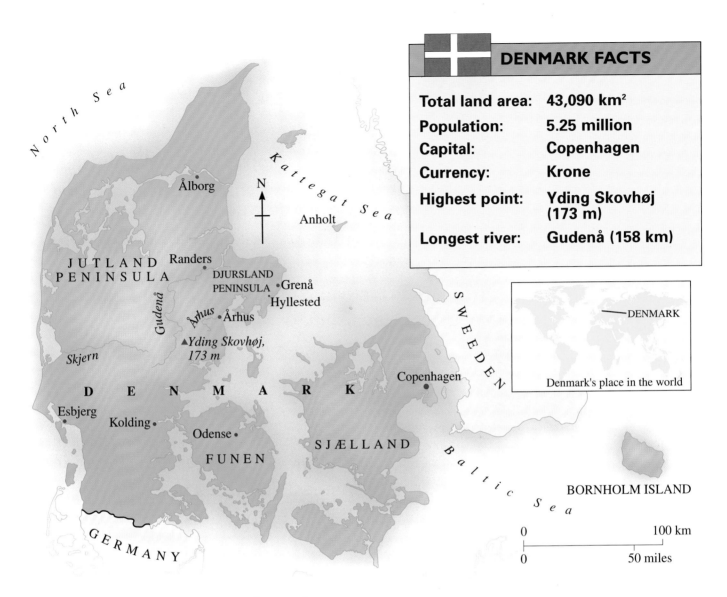

DENMARK FACTS

Total land area:	43,090 km²
Population:	5.25 million
Capital:	Copenhagen
Currency:	Krone
Highest point:	Yding Skovhøj (173 m)
Longest river:	Gudenå (158 km)

DENMARK

Denmark's place in the world

0 — 100 km

0 — 50 miles

Wealth in Denmark is shared out more evenly than in most countries, because people pay high taxes. Many workers pay more than 50 per cent of their wages in tax. The money is used to pay for a welfare system, which includes health care, benefits for the unemployed and the elderly, and public services. Compared to the rest of the world, it is difficult to become either very rich or very poor in Denmark.

▼ **Queen Margrethe II of Denmark on a visit to a seaside town. Denmark is the oldest monarchy in Europe.**

The city of Århus

Århus (pronounced 'Orhoose') is the second-largest city in Denmark after Copenhagen. The city first grew around the mouth of the Århus river, in about AD 900, during the Viking Age. The sheltered natural harbour made the site an ideal place for trade.

ÅRHUS'S NAME

The name 'Århus' comes from an early Danish word meaning 'river mouth'. In Danish, the letter 'Å' means a small river or a large stream. The city was named after its position at the mouth of the Århus river.

In the nineteenth century, manufacturing industries developed in the city, which provided work for many people. At the same time, a network of railways was built across Denmark, and Århus became an important railway centre.

Restaurants and cafés along the banks of the Århus river.

During the Second World War (1939–45), the German army occupied the city. After the war, one of the military airbases they had built was turned into the city airport.

▼ *Good national and international transport links are still very important to Århus. This train has just arrived from Hamburg, in Germany.*

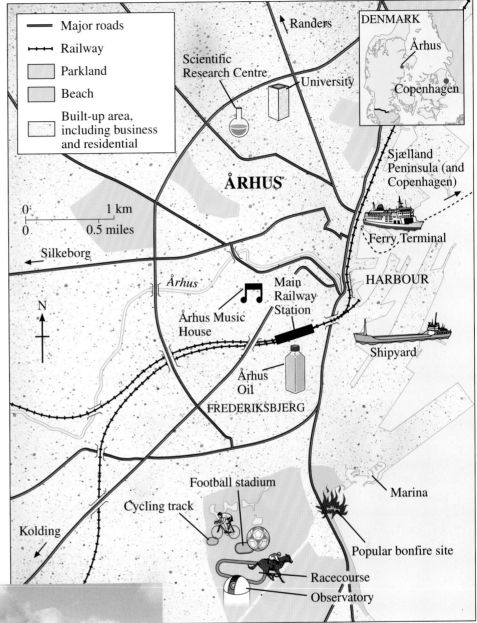

	Major roads
	Railway
	Parkland
	Beach
	Built-up area, including business and residential

DENMARK

Randers

Scientific Research Centre

University

Århus

Copenhagen

ÅRHUS

Sjælland Peninsula (and Copenhagen)

0   1 km
0   0.5 miles

Silkeborg

Ferry Terminal

Århus

HARBOUR

N

Main Railway Station

Århus Music House

Shipyard

Århus Oil

FREDERIKSBJERG

Football stadium

Cycling track

Kolding

Marina

Popular bonfire site

Racecourse

Observatory

By the 1930s, Århus had become a university town. Today it is one of the most important educational centres in Denmark, which helps to make Århus very attractive to young people. Many come from distant parts of Denmark to live and study in the city.

The village of Hyllested

The landscape around Hyllested is typically Danish, with cultivated farmland surrounding the village.

Hyllested (pronounced 'Hool-a-stur') is a small village set in beautiful countryside on the Djursland peninsula. The village is considered to be in a remote location by Danish standards, although Denmark is too small for anywhere to be very far from the outside world.

Sixty years ago, most people in Hyllested were employed in farming, or worked in the gravel pits near the village. Many worked in the fields of the nearby Rugård Estate. Most people rode the 3 km to the fields of Rugård on a bicycle.

HYLLESTED'S NAME

Hyllested's name can be traced back to the year 1183, when the village was known as *Hildir's sted*, meaning Hildir's place. Hildir was a Viking man's name.

The railway line that ran through the village made Hyllested a local centre for neighbouring farms and villages. There were shops, crafts and a mill. People could buy most of their daily needs in Hyllested, including clothes, shoes and all kinds of local foods. To children from neighbouring farms, Hyllested was 'the big town', where they went to take their farms' crops to the mill.

Today, only the houses are left in Hyllested – the railway line, the mill and every single shop are gone, as people's work has moved from the countryside to the cities. Rugård Estate is still a working farm, but most of the work is done using machinery rather than by hand, which means fewer people are needed. Many young people leave the village to search for jobs, or to go to college in the cities.

Hyllested village church. White churches are a typical feature of Danish villages. The oldest parts of this church are 800 years old.

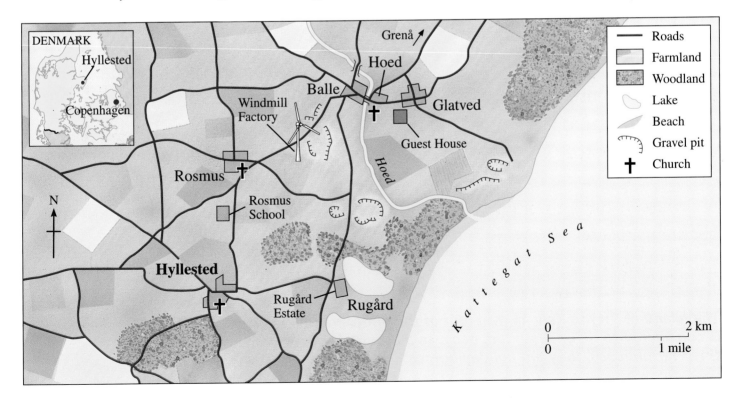

Land and climate

Denmark is a country of few extremes. Its landscape is made up of gently rolling hills, cultivated fields and a well-kept countryside. There are few wild, uncultivated areas, no volcanoes or earthquakes, few poisonous animals, and the landscape is one of the flattest in the world.

Denmark consists of a mainland peninsula, called the Jutland Peninsula, and 406 islands in all shapes and sizes, 325 of which are uninhabited. The many islands give Denmark a total coastline of 7,314 km.

The climate is influenced by Denmark's position between the North Sea and the Baltic Sea. Since there is nowhere in the country that is more than 75 km from the sea, there are few variations in climate between different places. Denmark is as far north as central Canada, but it seldom gets the same icy winters, although there are usually snowy days every year. In the summer, the sea is slow to heat up, which means summer days are often quite cool.

The island of Strynø Kalv, in the front of the photograph, is considered to be uninhabited, because although it has three farmhouses, they are holiday homes.

The most extreme form of Denmark's climate is its violent winds. In winter, occasional snowstorms can block roads and prevent people going to school or to work. When storms happen at the same time as high tides, there are sometimes floods. But such extremes are rare. Usually Danish children just hope for colder days and more snow in winter, and warmer weather for a trip to the beach in the summer.

▲ *This old tree was blow down by a storm in the early spring.*

◀ *Ice-skating on the lakes of Copenhagen. Some winters are so cold that the lakes and even the sea around the coast freeze.*

DENMARK'S CLIMATE		
Average daily temperature:		January: 0 °C
		July: 15.6 °C
Highest recorded temperature:	36 °C (1975)	
Lowest recorded temperature:	−32 °C (1982)	

Shaped by ice

The landscape around Århus was formed during the Ice Age, around 15,000 years ago. The city is surrounded by hills made of clay and gravel, which were pushed up by the huge glacier that once covered Denmark. The path of the Århus river was also carved out around this time, by streams of water running from the glacier.

Today Århus stretches out along a bay. Although the city is quite big, the countryside is not far from its outskirts, and there are several small forests nearby. People who live in Århus can combine the benefits of city life with easy access to woods, beaches and the countryside.

▼ Autumn colours in the forests of the wildlife park, just south of Århus.

City life changes greatly with the weather. Winters are often wet and grey. But when the snow comes, children in Århus make the most of it by skiing, sledging and having snowball fights in the city hills. Spring's warmer weather is always welcomed, and it brings people out in large numbers around the city squares and street cafés.

The hills around ▶ *Århus are ideal for sledging – on toboggans, trays or anything you can find!*

Since Denmark is so far north, there are longer summer days and lighter nights than in countries further south. It is traditional to celebrate the lightest summer nights by singing midsummer songs around huge bonfires. In Århus, a popular place for this is the beach just south of the marina, in Århus harbour.

▼ *A summer bonfire on the beach shortly after 10 pm. The sun has just set, but there will be a soft light on the northern horizon throughout the night.*

Life through four seasons

Hyllested, like Århus, is surrounded by hills formed during the Ice Age. The landscape is also made up of large deposits of stones and gravel. The area has a long tradition of gravel extraction from these deposits, where gravel is taken from pits and sold. The work used to be done by hand, but it is now mostly done using machinery. The gravel is used in road construction all over Djursland and further west in Jutland.

Farmers in Hyllested are affected much more by the changing seasons than city people, since the success of their crops is dependent on the weather conditions. Spring and early summer, from March to May, normally bring a fair amount of rain. This is the growing season in Denmark.

▼ *Gravel extraction in a pit just outside Hyllested.*

This ripe crop has ▶ *been flattened by a thunderstorm. Bad thunderstorms can reduce the value of a harvest by 50 per cent.*

14

Late summer should be warm and sunny, and this helps the crops to dry out before the harvest. But since the Danish weather is always changing, it is rarely as sunny as everyone would love it to be!

In winter snowstorms, Hyllested is occasionally cut off by snowdrifts, which block the roads leading to the village and make it impossible to drive cars through. The smaller roads leading to the village are always the last to be cleared when there is heavy snow, since the bigger, main roads, which are used by more traffic, have to be cleared first. If the village is cut off and someone is dangerously ill, or just about to have a baby, they are taken to hospital in armoured personnel carriers by the army.

▲ *An armoured personnel carrier sets out to rescue sick people in Hyllested who are blocked in by the snow.*

Home life

There have been great changes in family life in Denmark. Thirty-five years ago, most people lived in a household of at least three people. Today, 46 per cent of the population live either alone or in households of just two.

Denmark is a wealthy country, so most people have their own homes. Grandparents, parents and children rarely live in the same house. When elderly people can no longer cope with living on their own, they usually move to old people's homes, or to housing built specially for them. Most young people leave home at an early age and get their own flat. They finish their education while living with friends. In many towns, there are flats that have been built specially for young people. Most people don't marry until they are about 30 years old.

◀ *A typical Danish house being built with traditional red bricks, and (above) the finished house. Most people in Denmark live in detached family houses.*

FAVOURITE DANISH DISHES

Pastas, pizzas and burgers have become very popular with young Danes recently. But some traditional Danish dishes continue to be popular, too. Roast pork with brown gravy, boiled potatoes and carrots has long been considered the national dish. Meatballs with potato salad is another favourite, especially eaten outside in the garden. For lunch, most people eat open sandwiches of black bread with different meats, cheese or salad.

Arguments such as 'Who'll do the washing-up?' have been replaced by 'Who'll load the dishwasher?' – a third of all Danish families owns a dishwasher.

Another reason for the rising number of small households is the growing number of divorces. It is expected that at the turn of the twentieth century, a third of all Danish children will have experienced divorce in their family.

Most Danish homes are well equipped with luxury goods, such as a a television, a video-recorder and a washing machine. Many also have a spin-drier and a dishwasher. Computers have become very popular recently and soon, more than half of all Danish households will own at least one.

At home in Århus

Since 30,000 young people study in Århus, there is always a shortage of smaller homes for people living on their own. For many students, 'home' is a small, overpriced room. Camilla is an eighteen-year old student in Århus who grew up in a fishing village and left home when she was sixteen. She is lucky to have found a reasonable-sized place to live, with a 16 m² bedroom. She shares a bathroom and a kitchen with another girl in a similar room. Their rooms are in a modern, semi-detached house with a small garden. The only disadvantage is that it is quite far from the city centre.

'I love my home because I like making my own decisions, like tidying and cleaning up. I like visiting my parents in the village, but prefer to live on my own.' – Camilla Hjortshøj, 18 years old, student.

Camilla likes having her own place, where she has a large bedroom.

Students and old people in Århus tend to live close to the centre of the city, whereas most families with children live in modern flats or family houses in the fast-spreading suburbs. In the western parts of the city, there are areas of tall blocks of flats, where many refugees and immigrants have settled in recent years.

Closer to the city centre is an area with many small flats, called Frederiksbjerg. The flats were built about 100 years ago for workers and their families. Today, most of the flats are home to either students or the elderly. Some have shared toilets off the staircase, and a bath in the basement.

▲ *The Frederiksbjerg area, with typical Danish four- and five-storey houses.*

◄ *A Vietnamese immigrant buying vegetables in an Århus market.*

Home life in Hyllested

Hyllested today is in some ways like a suburb in a big city. People have their home there, but they shop and work in other places. Villagers can buy groceries and essentials in the villages of Balle or Tirstrup, a few kilometres away, but if they want anything more specialized, they have to drive to the larger towns of Grenå or Ebeltoft, over 15 km away.

Peter Vinther and Dorte Fleischer have a typical modern village family. They both grew up in Hyllested, and they like it so much they have decided to raise their own family there. Their house, like all the houses in the village, has a garden where they can keep rabbits and play with their dog. Peter and Dorte prefer their house to a flat in the city, which would have far less space.

▼ *Dorte Fleischer outside her family's house. Their house has lots of space for them to keep pets.*

Every morning, Dorte drives their three children, aged two, three and five, to kindergarten or daycare centres in the next village. Dorte and Peter are only able to get around in their cars, as it would be impossible to use public transport.

Everybody in Hyllested knows one another and the children always have somebody to visit. In that respect Hyllested is very different from the city.

'I would suffocate in a big city. I need the open spaces and fresh air. I think the village is a perfect place for my children to grow up in.'
– Dorte Fleischer, teacher.

▲ *A fruit stall on the village roadside. Shoppers help themselves and leave the money in the bucket.*

◀ *Dorte Fleischer having breakfast with her children.*

Denmark at work

Most Danes work an average of thirty-seven hours a week, in a wide range of different jobs. Denmark exports many of the goods it produces, which provides thousands of jobs selling many different products all over the world. The export trade is essential to pay for all the imported products, such as clothes, electronic equipment, tropical fruits, cars, timber and coal.

Fishing has always been an important industry to Denmark, since it is a coastal and island country. Today, most fish are used to produce fish meal and fish oil. Farming is also very important. Danish animal products, such as bacon and ham, are well known in many countries.

▼ *Svend Bilde learnt about fishing from his father. Today, an increased number of rules and regulations make life more difficult for fishermen. All of Svend's children have found jobs in other industries.*

Most Danes are employed in service jobs, such as banking, tourism and trade. In manufacturing, food processing is the largest sector. The production of machinery, chemical products and electronics is important too.

Today, it is common for both men and women to have full-time jobs. Jobs such as building are still mostly done by men. There are also jobs that are mainly done by women, such as nursing. However, more people every year are taking jobs that used to be done mostly by the other sex. So now, there are female builders and male nurses, for example.

Almost a third of all Danes aged between eighteen and sixty-six years old are not working. They are either unemployed, being paid a pension, or have taken part-paid leave to study or take care of their children.

TYPE OF WORK IN DENMARK

	Percentage of working population
Services:	66%
Manufacturing:	28%
Agriculture:	6%

▼ *Flight Sergeant I. M. Nielsen in the traffic-control tower.*

'I love aeroplanes and I've always wanted a job in aviation. Air-traffic control is exciting. I like working with the high-tech aviation equipment.' – Flight sergeant I.M. Nielsen, air-traffic controller.

Work in Århus

Every weekday morning, the roads leading into Århus are packed with cars bringing people to work. Over 35,000 people commute to the city every day, mostly by car, from villages and small towns surrounding Århus. They come to work in the 13,700 places of work in the city, from factories to shops and offices. There are both small and large companies, employing from one person to hundreds of people.

Lisbeth at work in one of the city's many bakeries.

TYPE OF WORK IN ÅRHUS, 1994	
	Percentage of working population
Services:	81%
Manufacturing:	17%
Other:	2%

'I'm still at high school, but I work in a bakery at weekends to earn pocket money. Most of my friends like to earn some money too.' – Lisbeth, 18 years old.

Århus Oil is a large company that produces vegetable oils. These are sold to seventy countries, including Australia and the USA. In the 1930s, Århus Oil was the biggest employer in Århus, but now only 600 people work there. This is because machines have taken over much of the work. Since the production of vegetable oils is a high-tech process, there are sixty people working just to develop new, specialized fats and oils. These may be used in sweets, cosmetics and lubricants.

▲ *The offices at Århus Oil, where business with seventy countries takes place.*

The harbour is an important place of work in Århus. More goods (apart from oil and coal) pass through Århus harbour than through any other in Denmark. Containers from all over the world can be seen on the busy quays. Since the end of the Cold War, in 1989, there has been a growing number of goods passing through the harbour on their way to Russia and the Baltic states.

▼ *A Russian tanker in Århus harbour.*

Work in Hyllested

'I feed most of my crops to chickens, which are sold to the Middle East. Everything is mechanized. About 180,000 chickens pass through the farm every year. It's just a small farm by modern standards.' – Poul Vinther, farmer (below).

Most work in Hyllested used to be in farming, but farm machinery now does many of the jobs traditionally done by hand. Today, only about a quarter of the villagers work in farming, and the farms are much bigger than they used to be.

The farms are mainly animal farms, keeping pigs and cows, and most of their crops are used for animal feed. The animals are used to produce bacon, ham and cheese, which are sold abroad to countries such as Britain, Germany, the USA and Japan.

A combine harvester in the fields around Hyllested.

There are a growing number of small businesses in Hyllested. These rely on modern technology and communications, such as computers and fax machines, to be able to carry out business in a village. One business designs office furniture to be sold to Germany. There is also a small factory producing accessories for dogs, such as collars, leads and baskets.

Henning Kjærgaard at the Nordtank wind-turbine factory, checking parts for a wind turbine that will be sold to India.

Other people from Hyllested work as teachers, doctors, or in other public service jobs, but mostly in nearby towns, such as Grenå. They rely on their cars to get them to work every day.

The largest factory near the village is the Nordtank wind-turbine factory, which is in the middle of farmland just outside Hyllested. Wind turbines provide an alternative source of power in Denmark, since massive public protests over twenty years ago prevented nuclear power stations being built. This inspired companies like Nordtank to develop wind turbines for the production of electricity. Ninety per cent of the turbines from Nordtank are exported to seventeen countries around the world.

Going to school

Danish children start school when they are five or six years old. They then belong to the same class, in the same school, for the next ten years, until they are sixteen. Each class has its own class teacher, who has a close relationship with pupils and their parents. This relationship is very important in Danish schools. Sometimes classes have the same teacher for the whole ten years at school. At the age of sixteen, children take an exam before going to high school for three years, either to prepare for university, or to train in a practical skill or trade.

School starts at 8 am. There are no school uniforms and children address their teacher by their first name. Children under ten years old have four or five lessons a day and finish at about 12 pm, while older children have lessons until about 2 pm. Lunch breaks are only ten minutes long, which is just enough time to eat a sandwich brought from home. Danish schools do not have canteens, so all the children bring packed lunches to school.

Most younger children stay at school in a special playroom until their parents collect them later in the day.

Children arriving at school by bicycle. Many children ride their bicycle to school.

MAIN SCHOOL SUBJECTS

Danish	Geography
Maths	Music
English	Art
German	Crafts
Science	Cookery
History	Physical Education

▲ *Girls grind flour the way people did in the Iron Age, in a practical history workshop. This way, they experience Iron-Age living for themselves.*

Playrooms are important to parents, because in most Danish families both parents have full-time jobs.

It has always been considered important in Denmark for children to learn practical skills. As well as subjects like geography, maths and history, both boys and girls study woodwork, crafts and cookery. Big school trips, called 'camp school', are usually organized by the class teacher once every fourth year, with smaller trips two or three times a year. These trips are very popular with the children.

Lunch at school ▶ usually consists of open sandwiches on black bread, which children bring with them from home.

University City

Århus has many schools and colleges, and many young people go to university there. Most children go to the fifty-one state schools in the city, which have up to 780 pupils each. In recent years, Århus has spent less money on schools than other large towns, which means the schools now offer slightly fewer lessons and less support for children with learning difficulties. This has been particularly difficult for schools in the western parts of Århus, where the children of some immigrants speak poor Danish when they start school.

Cookery is a popular subject in the sixth grade at Risskov School. In this picture, Kasper (below right) and Søren are preparing Danish meatballs.

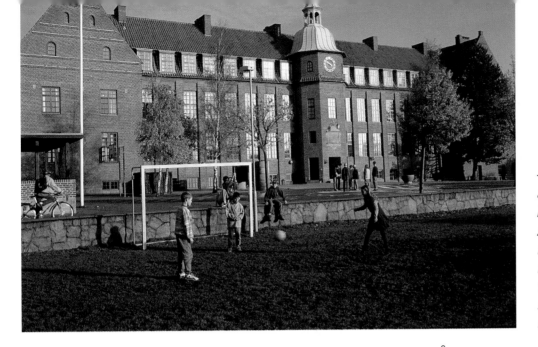

◀ *Risskov School has a very good reputation, but like many other Århus schools, it now needs money for more modern workshops to teach practical subjects such as woodwork and cookery.*

There are a number of private schools in Århus that specialize in the teaching of music, the arts or religion. These schools have been opened by parents who want a more specialist education for their child, or who are worried about the quality of education in government schools. They pay 20 per cent of the costs, while the government pays the rest.

At Århus University and at the many different colleges in the city, students can study almost any subject, from history or music, to dentistry, nursing or business studies. Århus is the only place in Denmark where students can study journalism, and the theatre offers drama courses.

'When I finish school, I want to study physiotherapy. But I may change my mind because Århus has an endless choice of courses.' – Camilla Hjortshøj, 18 years old (left).

School in Hyllested

There have been no schools in Hyllested since 1961, when the village school was closed down because there were not enough children in the village to attend it. That year, the schools in four other villages closed down and a larger, central school, the Rosmus School, was built in the middle of the farmland, 2 km north of Hyllested. About 350 children go to the Rosmus School, taking a bus from several villages and farms in the area. Concentrating the children in a larger school makes it possible to have better modern equipment, such as computers and electric guitars for music lessons.

The fourteen children in Class 6A come from six different villages, including Hyllested.

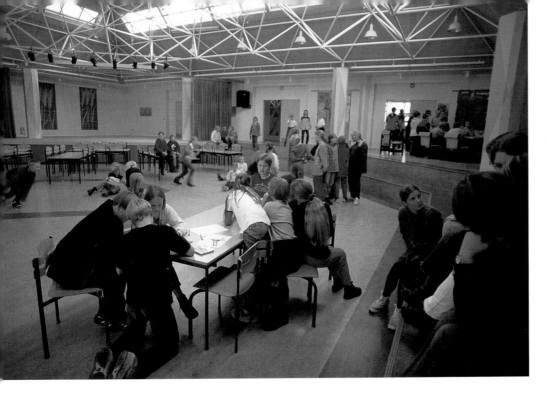

◀ The school hall during a break between lessons. Some children are playing games, while others are drawing or just talking.

▼ Rosmus School has been using computers in daily lessons for many years.

Children at Rosmus School study the main school subjects that are taught in all Danish schools. Five times a year they can also spend one week studying a particular theme or subject. Another tradition is the annual sports day. This includes a challenging triathlon race (a combination of swimming, running and cycling).

Once a year, a large party is held and a school play is staged. The choir and other musical groups put on a concert every spring. Rosmus School shows that in modern Denmark, village schools are as good as city schools.

Denmark at play

Most Danes enjoy five weeks' holiday a year, as well as weekends, to relax and pursue their hobbies and interests. Many people join a club to share a sport or hobby. Sports are very popular, especially football, gymnastics and badminton. The two major sports associations in Denmark include over 10,000 sports clubs, with a total of 3 million members.

DANISH PUBLIC HOLIDAYS	
New Year's Day	1 Jan
Easter	March/April
Great Prayer Day	April/May
Ascension Day	May/June
Whit Monday	May/June
Constitution Day	5 June
Christmas Day	25 December
Boxing Day	26 December

Fishing in the early spring on a canal at Sivested, central Djursland. Fishing is a popular pastime all over Denmark.

Many Danes like to travel abroad for their holidays. In 1994, over 1.4 million package holidays were sold in Denmark. Many families and young people also went abroad independently, so a very large percentage of the population leaves the country every year. The Mediterranean has been a popular place to go on holiday for many years. Places such as the USA, the Far East and Australia, are also becoming popular.

▲ *A family waits to board the ferry to Anholt Island (see the map on page 5), at the start of a cycling holiday.*

Christmas is the most important festival of the year in Denmark. Streets and shops are decorated from the middle of November, and on Christmas Eve (24 December), families gather together for a big Christmas dinner. Another Danish tradition is to walk around the Christmas tree on Christmas Eve singing carols. On Christmas Day and Boxing Day, the country almost comes to a standstill as everybody relaxes and eats more!

▼ *A traditional Danish Christmas Day lunch.*

Leisure time in Århus

'I play football at least three days a week. I like playing music too, but right now sports are number one.' – Kasper, 12 years old.

Kasper and his twin brother Niklas practise football.

There are lots of different ways to relax and have fun in Århus. The city has more than 500 clubs and associations, dealing with hobbies from stamp-collecting to flying model aircrafts.

Sports are very popular in Århus, and the city has one of the best football teams in Denmark, called AGF. This is a great inspiration to young football players, like twelve-year-olds Kasper and Niklas, who play in one of the smaller clubs around the city.

◀ *A mock battle at the annual Viking Market in Århus.*

Århus has several theatres and a very active music scene. Some of the best Danish rock bands come from Århus, and many people consider Århus to be the most interesting city in Denmark. People in Copenhagen would probably disagree though!

▼ *Street performances like this one are popular during the Århus Festival Week.*

Århus is the home of several festivals during the year. The most famous is the annual Festival Week, in early autumn, which has a new theme every year and attracts performers and audiences from all over Denmark and abroad. Another annual festival is the Viking Market, which takes place over a long weekend in late July, on the beach

and in the forests south of Århus. At this festival, people dress, trade, work and even fight as the Vikings used to, a thousand years ago. Mock battles have rules that make sure nobody is hurt, but they look very dramatic.

Leisure time in Hyllested

Hyllested does not have the vast number of leisure activities that Århus has. But many activities are within a short drive away, in the nearby villages of Balle, Tirstrup and Rosmus. The drive is no longer than the journey from the suburbs of Århus to reach activities in the city's centre.

The Hyllested Village Association organizes talks by famous people on different topics, especially travel. The annual sports festival takes place every summer. It includes events such as aerobics, athletics, football and rounders, in which both children and their parents compete. There are also various concerts by visiting orchestras in the village throughout the year. The Hyllested Hunting Association organizes talks, education, hunts and club evenings for its members.

▼ *Children at the local music school in the village.*

▼ *Children practise for the annual village rock festival.*

Julie and Ditte visiting their horses after school. Keeping animals is popular with children in Hyllested, where there is more space than in Århus.

Two scout groups, which meet in Balle and Tirstrup villages, are very popular with the children in Hyllested. The groups, which have both boy and girl members, learn how to sleep outdoors, cook on campfires and build rafts. Once a year they go on a camping trip. The scouts also collect materials such as glass and paper for recycling.

Some children go to an evening class at Rosmus School, where they can choose from lots of different courses, from learning how to play a musical instrument, to doing gymnastics.

Apart from organized activities, children in Hyllested also like to entertain themselves by visiting each other after school. They watch television, listen to music, or play in their gardens or the woods nearby.

EVENING CLASSES AT ROSMUS SCHOOL

French	Basketball
Fashion	Accountancy
Tractor driving	Psychology
Flower arranging	Hunting
Rock music	Fishing
Horse keeping	Leather crafts
Cookery	Moto-cross

Evening classes are popular all over Denmark. They are a chance to learn something new and meet people at the same time. Classes are free for young people, and only a small fee for adults.

The future

Denmark has problems like every other country. There are homeless people living on the streets, and families who are frustrated by being unemployed for a long time. Some hospitals have long waiting lists, and not all old people receive the care they need. But most people in Denmark are living a life that their grandparents could only dream of. Compared to the early 1980s, Danes are buying 25 per cent more clothes, cars, furniture, holidays and many other products.

Most people now get financial help from the government in one way or another, such as payment of their medical and dental costs, or child-support benefits.

A male nurse visiting an old man in his garden.

The government spends almost half its money on providing benefits. Most people agree that the benefits system is too expensive, and that it will have to change.

The big question facing Danes is how to maintain their standard of living. A Dane's hourly wage is the same as the wage for ninety hours' work in China or India. To keep this high hourly wage, Denmark must continue to produce and sell good designs and products, which are popular in other countries, despite their fairly high price.

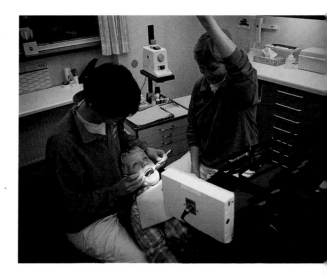

▲ *Anders Sørensen has his teeth checked at school. All children in Denmark have free dental care, which is usually provided at school.*

RISING STANDARD OF LIVING

Percentage of children aged 7–15 with electronic equipment in their bedrooms		
	1987	1993
Radio	91%	96%
CD/record player	32%	66%
Tape recorder	88%	95%
Television	27%	62%
Computer	18%	32%

▼ *Scandinavian Airlines (a joint Danish, Norwegian and Swedish company) faces stiff competition from other airlines because its staff's high wages mean the fares are high.*

The future of Århus

People in Århus are confident of a prosperous future for the city. In recent years, Århus has grown richer more quickly than the Danish average. A newspaper that started in the city is now Denmark's biggest, employing more than 1,000 people. The city has been chosen as the home of a centre to develop 'green' technology in Danish cities.

The Århus Music House has been a huge success. Centrally located on top of a hill near the city hall, it has helped to show the musical importance of the city. Here, people can listen to the City Symphony Orchestra, local rock and jazz bands, international superstars or even large-scale operas.

A children's festival in front of the Århus Music House.

A large amount of money was spent on the Music House. Some people thought too much was spent, but the local government thought the Music House would be good for the city. They argued that it would attract new visitors, students and businesses. All these help the city grow in many ways.

Århus is twinned with cities in Norway and Sweden, as are many towns in Denmark, but Århus is also twinned with St Petersburg in Russia and Harbin in China. Both are a long way from Århus, but the city is always trying to develop international links.

ÅRHUS'S POPULATION

	Population
1901	98,016
1960	221,895
1995	277,477

Århus is continuing to grow in population as business, industry and education attract people to the city.

'Co-operation is the key to our success in Århus. Scientists, engineers, businessmen and trade unions have managed to work together to create new ideas and new business.' – Thorkild Simonsen, Lord Mayor of Århus.

The future of Hyllested

'I expect to get even more work in the future. The months leading up to Christmas are especially busy, but there is work to be done in forests all year round.'
– Peter Vinther, freelance forestry worker.

There have been many changes in Hyllested over the last fifty years, and the village is still changing. Depopulation is a problem in villages all over the world. Some survive by becoming tourist attractions, which tends to make them overcrowded for part of the year and almost empty at other times. Hyllested, on the other hand, is developing new, modern businesses.

One new business is Birgitte Lyngsø's design company, which is situated in her home, in a typical, half-timbered village house. Birgitte designs

Peter Vinther (left) netting Christmas trees with his Scottish friend Steven, who has come over to Denmark to work in the busy time leading up to Christmas.

children's clothes and toys. One of her latest designs is a set of medieval costumes, to be sold in Britain and Germany. Her clothes are tested on local children, to spot weak points or improvements that are needed. They are then made in other parts of Denmark and abroad, and sold in several countries.

Other people in Hyllested work at home too. There is another clothes designer and a freelance journalist in the village, and they both do business with companies a long way away.

Hyllested's survival in the future will depend on telecommunications, such as computers and fax machines, and modern transport. They will mean that people in Hyllested and other villages in Denmark will be able to continue to enjoy living and working in a village.

▲ *Birgitte Lyngsø tests two of her medieval costumes at an early stage of their design.*

HYLLESTED'S POPULATION

	Population
1901	506
1960	575
1995	430

Hyllested's population has decreased since 1960, as people have moved to towns and cities for jobs.

▼ *The arrival of families with young children is a sign that Hyllested will continue to be an active village community.*

Glossary

Armoured personnel carrier A military vehicle usually used to transport troops in a war zone.

Cold War The rivalry that existed between the USSR and the USA from the end of the 1940s until the late 1980s.

Commute Travel between a person's home and their place of work.

Depopulation A reduction in the number of people living in a place.

Dialects Variations of language according to different regions.

European Union (EU) A group of fifteen European countries, made up of Denmark, France, Germany, Britain, Italy, Ireland, Sweden, Finland, Austria, Spain, Portugal, Greece, the Netherlands, Belgium and Luxembourg, who are working together for the interests of Europe.

Freelance A person who is usually self-employed, offering services on a temporary basis.

'Green' technology A process using products that do as little harm to the environment at possible.

Ice Age A period in history, which ended about 10,000 BC, when the earth's climate was much colder.

Immigrant A person who has moved from their own country to live permanently in another country.

Iron Age A period in history, from 500 BC to AD 700, when iron was the most important raw material for producing tools and weapons.

Military airbase Airfield from which military aeroplanes operate.

Mock battles Pretend battles in which the participants try to make it look realistic.

Monarchy A form of government with a sovereign, such as a king or queen at the head.

Package holidays A holiday that includes all the arrangements in the price.

Peninsula A piece of land almost surrounded by water, or which sticks out far into a sea or lake.

Public service jobs Jobs paid for by the government, such as teaching, tax collecting, dentistry and medicine.

Refugee A person who has left their own country to seek safety elsewhere.

Welfare system A system where help is given by the government to people who need it, such as the aged and the unemployed.

Suburbs Districts on the edge of a large town or city.

Taxes Money paid by citizens to the government.

Telecommunications Communication over a distance by cable, using equipment such as telephones and faxes.

Further information

Books to Read

Continents: Europe by Ewan McLeish (Wayland, 1996)

Into Europe: Life in Europe by Deborah Elliott (Wayland, 1994)

Into Europe: The Environment by Deborah Elliott (Wayland, 1994)

Modern Industrial World: Sweden by Bo Kage Carlsson (Wayland, 1995)

Real World: European Union by Chris Durbin (Watts, 1995)

Sources

The statistics in this book came from the following sources:
Statistisk Årbog, 1995 (Danmarks Statistik, 1996); *Århus 1996 – Statistical information*; Ebeltoft Kommune.

Picture acknowledgements

All photographs, except page 25 (top), are by Ole Steen Hansen. Page 25 (top): Århus Oil.
All maps are by Hardlines.
Border artwork is by Kate Davenport.

Index

Page numbers in **bold** refer to photographs.